CW00972793

Living in the light

100 prayers for young people

David Adam

kevin
mayhew

First published in 2008 by

KEVIN MAYHEW LTD
Buxhall, Stowmarket, Suffolk, IP14 3BW
E-mail: info@kevinmayhewltd.com
Website: www.kevinmayhew.com

9 8 7 6 5 4 3 2 1 0

ISBN 978 1 84867 024 2
Catalogue No. 1501104

Design by Chris Coe
Edited by Katherine Laidler
Illustrations by Melody-Anne Lee & Air Design

Printed and bound in the EU

Contents

Introduction

We live in a wonderful world that presents us with many choices. There are so many things we can enjoy and do. We have to make definite choices: we choose what we eat and what we wear; we choose what we watch on television, what games we play and who our friends are. In all our choices we make sure that our bodies and our minds are looked after. It would be sad if our body starved or our mind remained empty. In the same way, it is important that our inner being – our spirit – is cared for properly. To be fully healthy we need to care for our body, mind and spirit.

For our spirit to grow fully, we need a relationship with God. One of the saints said to God, 'To turn away from you is to enter darkness.' The choice is ours: we can choose to live in a world without knowing God or we can learn of his love and his power. To choose to live in the dark seems foolish when the Light of God is offered to us. God – Father, Son and Holy Spirit – seeks to be our friend. But we can only truly be friends if we spend time with each other, talk to each other and express our love for each other. We can do this by setting aside some time each day to remind ourselves of the love and presence of God. The more we become aware of God and his love, the more we are able to venture and be fully alive. It is like coming out of the darkness and walking in the light.

To help you in this adventure, I offer these prayers for you to use. They are not to replace your own words but rather to help you to see how great God is and how to speak to him. It is a good idea to use the same prayer for a while, until the words become your own. Do not rush from sentence to sentence but spend some time allowing the full meaning of the words to enter your heart. Use one of these prayers each day, or even for a week. Use the words to make you aware of the reality behind them: God is with you and loves you. In this way you begin to live in the Light of God.

Once you know you have this light, you will be able to pass it on to friends – not so much by your words but by the fullness of life that they see you living. You will become a torch bearer for God.

God bless you and fill your life with his love and light.

Jesus Comes
(Christmas)

Lord, awaken me to your love.
Make me aware that you come to me
today and every day.
Help me to rejoice in your coming
and in your abiding presence.
Amen.

Thank you, Lord God,
that what was secret for many ages
has been made known to all.
I give you thanks for the Word made flesh,
that Jesus has been born in Bethlehem
and told us of your love,
Amen.

God, I rejoice in your greatness
for you are wonderful.
I give thanks that you sent your Son
to be our Saviour.
May I be prepared for his coming.
Amen.

Lord God, as Mary and Joseph said 'Yes' to you
and did your will,
help me to work
for the coming of your kingdom
and to serve you.
Amen.

Glory to you, O God,
in sending your Son into the world.
Help me to see your glory as revealed in Jesus
and to seek to show your glory to others.
Amen.

God, who by the leading of a star
brought the wise men to Jesus,
guide me in my life
and bring me to give my love to you.
Amen.

God, thank you
that you have revealed your love for all people,
in all places and at all times.
I can find you wherever I am
and know that you are with me
and that you care for me.
Amen.

Jesus, you came into the world
to be our Saviour.
Thank you that you became a child of earth
so that I may become a child of God.
Amen.

Awaken me, O God, to your coming.
Open my eyes that I may see you.
Open my ears that I may hear you.
Open my lips that I may talk about you.
Touch my heart that I may love you.
Come, Lord, come.
Amen.

The risen Lord
(Easter)

God, thank you for those who have told me
the Good News of your love
and that Jesus is risen from the dead.
As I know the risen Christ,
let me tell others about this wonderful miracle.
Amen.

Jesus, my Lord and my God,
let me rejoice in the resurrection;
let me know you now by faith.
Jesus, I give thanks to you
for life and life eternal.
Amen.

Lord God, to you be praise
for through your Son Jesus Christ
you have conquered death
and opened the way to eternal life.
I rejoice in your love
and in the resurrection of your Son.
Alleluia.
Amen.

Jesus, thank you
for the power of the resurrection
and the courage you give to your people.
Help me to know I am never alone
but that you are with me always
as my friend and Saviour.
Amen.

CHRIST IS
ALIVE
ALLELUIA!

Lord Jesus, in you is life
and life eternal.
I put my trust and my hope in you
for with you is life and love.
To you be glory and praise
for ever and ever.
Amen.

I give you praise and glory, Lord God,
for you give us the seasons:
a time for sowing and a time for reaping,
a time for burying seeds
and a time for watching them rise.
Help me to understand the power
of the death and resurrection of Jesus.
Amen.

Lord Jesus, who in a wonderful sacrament
has left us a memorial of your life offered
and of your death and passion,
help me to understand and respect
this wonderful mystery
and to know the joy of your resurrection
and your presence with us.
Amen.

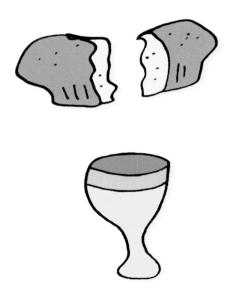

Creator of all things

Lord, the earth is yours and all that is in it.
All things come from you.
Help me to love the world
with the love that you have for the world
and to give glory to you
for all that I have each day.
Amen.

God, you are the Creator of all things.
You give us life and this world to live in.
Help me to use all to your glory
and to the benefit of your creation.
Amen.

Lord God, as you give freely to me,
teach me to be free in my giving.
I pray that the resources of the world
may not be hoarded or squandered
but used for the benefit of all.
Amen.

Creator God,
thank you for the wonder of creation.
I pray that I may use the resources of the world
to the benefit of others
and in the care of our planet.
Make me sensitive and caring
in my dealings with others,
that we may learn through each other
of your great love.
Amen.

Lord Jesus, teach me to love the world
with the love that you have for the world.
May I learn to care for others
and help any who are in need,
for as much as I do it to the least
I do it to you.
Amen.

Lord God, you have created a world
where there is enough for everyone's needs
but not for everyone's greed.
Help me not to damage
or squander your creation
but to share with others.
Amen.

Lord God, thank you
that you have made the world
and all that is in it.
I rejoice in your love and protection.
Help me to trust in you
and to know you are with me always.
Amen.

Lord, you have given us a rich world
where there is enough for everyone.
Help us who have received plenty
to be generous with others
and so express your care for all.
Amen.

Giver of life

Creator God,
thank you for the gift of life
and for the wonders and mystery
of your world.
Help me to use what you have given me
to your glory and the benefit of all.
I ask this through your Son,
Jesus Christ, my Saviour.
Amen.

God, thank you for giving us life
and making each one of us special.
May I use the talents you have given me
to your glory and to the benefit of others.
Amen.

God, you have given me many good things;
my life is rich because of you.
Help me to be generous with what I have
and to be willing to give to others.
Amen.

Glory to you, O God,
for you provide my daily needs.
You have made me for yourself
and I hunger for your love
until I come to your presence.
In you alone am I truly refreshed
and restored to the fullness of life.
Glory to you, O God.
Amen.

Peace be
with you

God of love

Good and glorious God,
you have made me out of your love
and for your love.
Touch my heart with the joy of your presence,
that I may give myself in love to you.
Amen.

Lord God, you are a generous and loving God,
giving us more than we deserve.
You are full of compassion,
slow to anger and of great kindness.
Help me to work for you
and to do your will out of love and joy.
Amen.

Father God, thank you for your love
and for the love in my home.
Help me to show your love and kindness
to others
and to remember you are with me every day.
Amen.

God, I rejoice in your love for me.
I seek to love you with my whole being:
with my heart, my mind,
my soul and my strength.
As you love me
help me to learn to love you better
and to love others.
Amen.

Lord God, you give me your love
and count me as one of your children.
Help me to give my love to you
and to reveal your love for others
through my actions and words.
Amen.

Lord God, you have created me out of love
and for your love.
You ask me to show your love to all,
as you love everyone.
Help me to learn to love those who are against me,
even when I cannot love their actions.
Amen.

Lord God, I rejoice in your love
for me and for all people.
May I learn to reveal your love
in my dealings with others
and so help to bring them to know and love you.
Amen.

Prince of Peace

Lord Jesus,
help me to know you as the Prince of Peace
and to accept your rule in my heart
and in my life.
Teach me to pray and live by the words
'Your will be done'.
Amen.

Lord Jesus,
guide me into the way of peace.
I give my hands to work for you.
Let my feet always be on your path.
Let me speak your praises and do your will
this day and for ever.
Amen.

Lord Jesus, let your peace fill my heart,
my actions and my days.
Let your peace be known in my life
and in everything I do.
Help me to be an instrument of your peace
and to share your peace with others.
Amen.

Wonderful Jesus

Lord Jesus, you are the Son of God,
the Promised One.
You are Christ our Saviour.
As you give yourself for me and to me,
help me to give my life and love to you.
Amen.

Jesus, you just need to speak the word
and people are healed.
Thank you for the words of the Bible,
especially the Gospels.
More than anything, thank you
that you are the Word made flesh.
Amen.

Jesus Christ, Light of the World,
scatter the darkness from about me
and within me
and help me to walk as a child of the light.
Help me to know that you love me
and are with me always.
Amen.

Jesus, Son of God, Saviour,
I put my trust in you
and in your almighty power.
You are able to bring light to my darkness
and rescue me when I cannot help myself.
Jesus, help me to know you better
and to love you more.
Amen.

Lord Jesus,
friend of the friendless
and help of the helpless,
I come to you in faith.
I trust in you, in your love and in your power.
Lord Jesus, help me to hear your call
and to follow you.
Amen.

Father, thank you for Jesus the Good Shepherd;
through his death he has destroyed death,
and by his rising to life again
he has opened for us the gate of glory.
May I know his love and protection in my life.
I ask this through Jesus Christ my Lord.
Amen.

Lord, giver of life and love,
thank you for the water that refreshes
and revives us.
Thank you for Jesus, the Water of Life,
who gives us life eternal.
Amen.

Lord Jesus, you are the Good Shepherd.
You seek and save the lost.
You care for the fallen and restore the sick.
You call each of us by our name
and you offer us eternal life.
Lord, help me to know you
and to follow you day by day.
Amen.

Lord Jesus, you bring healing to the ill,
strength to the weak
and love to the lonely.
Help me to care for all who are in need
and be grateful for all that I have.
Amen.

Jesus, you are able to change
emptiness into fullness
and to turn lives from wickedness
and wastefulness
into goodness and usefulness.
Bless my life with your presence and power.
Amen.

God, thank you for the faithfulness of your word
and for Jesus, the Word made flesh.
May I find in him the way to life eternal.
Amen.

Jesus, I welcome you as my King and Saviour.
Take my heart and fill it with your love.
Take my mind and work through it.
Take my will and act through it.
Take my life and make it yours.
As you give yourself to me,
I give myself to you,
Christ my King and my God.
Amen.

Jesus, you are the Christ, the Son of God.
You came to our world and became human
so that you could lift us into your kingdom
and let us share in the Divine.
Thank you for your love
and your abiding presence with me.
Amen.

Lord Jesus, thank you that you have shown
the love and the forgiveness of the Father.
I think you are great and do wonderful things.
Amen.

Lord Jesus, you are my King.
Come and rule in my heart
that your kingdom may come in me.
Lord, I give thanks to you
for you are my Saviour.
Amen.

Lord, you are my shepherd,
my protector and my guardian.
You have given your life
that I can have life eternal.
You will lead me into the way of peace
if only I will follow you.
I thank you for your love and sacrifice for me.
Amen.

Come, Holy Spirit

Lord, I wait for you.
Come, Holy Spirit.
Lord, take away my fear.
Come, Holy Spirit.
Lord, give me the courage to proclaim your Gospel.
Come, Holy Spirit.
Lord, fill my life with your power.
Come, Holy Spirit.
Lord, teach me patience as I wait.
Come, Holy Spirit.
Amen.

Come, Holy Spirit of God,
fill my life with your presence,
strengthen me through your power
and guide me in your goodness.
May my life show
that you are with me and within me always.
Amen.

Come, Holy Spirit of God, fill me with your love.
Come, Holy Spirit of God, fill me with your power.
Come, Holy Spirit of God, fill me with your light.
Come, Holy Spirit of God,
fill me with your inspiration.
Then may I bring others to know you
and to love you.
Amen.

Father, Son and Holy Spirit

Glory be to the Father
and to the Son
and to the Holy Spirit,
as it was in the beginning,
is now
and shall be for ever.
Amen.

Glory to you, Father,
for you have created me out of your love.
May I live to your glory.
Glory to you, Jesus, Son of God,
for you have redeemed me by your love.
May I share in your saving work.
Glory to you, Holy Spirit,
for you refresh and restore me
through your love.
May I walk before you in newness of life.
Glory for ever to you, Father, Son and Holy Spirit.
Amen.

Father, you are here with me and I love you.
Jesus, you are here with me and I love you.
Spirit, you are here with me and I love you.
Amen.

Father, Creator and giver of life,
I come to you in love.
I worship and adore you.
Jesus Christ, Saviour and rescuer from death,
I come to you in love.
I worship and adore you.
Holy Spirit, Guide and giver of power,
I come to you in love.
I worship and adore you.
Blessing and praise to you, Holy Three,
glorious Trinity.
Amen.

Jesus ever with us

God, I know the sun is there
on the cloudiest of days.
Help me to know that Jesus is always with me.
He is ready to hear my prayers and to help me.
Lord Jesus, thank you for being with me
and for praying for me.
Amen.

Abide with me, Lord,
abide with me today and for ever.
Abide with me in my joys and my sorrows.
Abide with me in darkness and light.
Abide with me, and your whole Church.
Abide with me in time and eternity.
Amen.

Lord Jesus, thank you for becoming one with us
and sharing our joys and sorrows.
Help me to know you are always with me
and let me not lose my awareness of you
through neglect or busyness.
Amen.

Lord Jesus,
I do not know what might happen to me,
I do not know where I might have to go,
but I do know you are with me
and you will guide me
on my journey through life.
Lord Jesus, as you seek to be my friend,
let me welcome you each day.
Amen.

Christ is with me, Christ is before me,
Christ is behind me, Christ is within me,
Christ is beneath me, Christ is above me,
Christ on my right and on my left.
Christ all around me and within.

Called by Jesus

Lord Jesus, as you called the fishermen
and they obeyed you,
help me to do what you would have me do
and to seek to be the person you would have me be.
Amen.

Jesus, as you came to the disciples,
you come to me.
You want me to be your friend
and to help in the work that you do.
Jesus, I ask that I might be a true friend
and know that you are with me always.
Amen.

Lord Jesus,
as you love all and care for all,
may I share in your healing and caring ministry.
Make me aware of those in need
and how I can help.
Amen.

Risen Lord, may I know that you are with me
and seek to be my friend.
Help me to give time and attention
to you each day,
that I may share in your mission
and do what you would have me do.
Amen .

Lord Jesus, may I know you
and, in knowing you, love you,
and, in loving you, proclaim you,
that it may be known I believe in you
and that you are with me always.
Amen.

Lord Jesus,
take my hands and work with them;
take my feet and reach others through them;
take my lips and speak through them;
take my heart and set it on fire
with love for you and for all people.
Amen.

Jesus, thank you that you have called me
to know you and to enjoy your presence.
Give me the wisdom and the courage
to proclaim the Good News
and tell of your saving power.
Amen.

Lord, thank you that you have called me
to be the salt of the earth.
Help me to work to improve my life
and the area in which I live.
May I show that it is a joy
to be alive and to know you.
Amen.

Lord, you have called me
to share in your ministry of love and care.
You reveal yourself to me in the cry
of the poor and needy.
Help me to be open and generous in my life
and know that when I care for the least of these
I am showing my love for you,
Jesus Christ my Lord.
Amen.

Loving Father, help me to listen carefully
to the call of Jesus.
Give me a love for him that sends me out
to tell others of his power and his greatness.
May I share in his mission and in his message
by the way I live and speak.
Amen.

God, you made me to love and obey you.
Help me to do what is right
and to stand against evil;
to show my love for you
by the way I care for others
and the world around me.
Amen.

Lord Jesus, you have called me
to work for you and with you.
Help me to be faithful to you,
to work against evil
and to seek to do what is right and good.
May I be ready to stand up
for all who strive for goodness and peace.
I ask this in your power and in your name,
Jesus Christ my Lord.
Amen.

God, you have called me to work with you
and to do good for the world.
Protect me from all evil
and keep me in the right way
today and always.
Amen.

Jesus, help me to shine with love for you
and by my life show that I know you
and love you.
May I share with others
the love that you give to me.
Amen.

Lord God, you have called me
to be one of your people,
to give my life to you
and in the service of others.
As you have called me,
strengthen me
and make me worthy of my calling.
Amen.

Lord Jesus, you have called me
to be your apostle
and to go out and tell others of you.
Give me strength and wisdom to do this
and help me to know
that you are with me always.
Amen.

Lord God, you have called me
to follow you and to belong to you in love.
Help me to show your love to all people.
Send me out
to tell of your presence and your kingdom
in the world.
Amen.

Lord Jesus, you have called me
to be the salt of the earth.
Help me to fight quietly against evil
and to encourage people to enjoy life.
Let me show I belong to you
and that you give me the gift of life eternal.
Amen.

When we are troubled

Lord God,
you know I am often in the midst of troubles
and there are dangers all around.
Keep me in the protection of your love
and in the life which is eternal.
Amen.

Holy and strong God, I trust in you.
Help me to stand against all evil
and to seek to tell others of your goodness.
Give me courage in troubles
but, above all, help me to know
you are always with me.
I ask this in the name of Jesus
who died and rose again.
Amen.

Lord, I come in darkness to your light.
I come in weakness to your strength.
I come in sadness to your joy.
I come in trouble to your peace.
I come in weariness to be renewed.
Lord, change me and I shall be changed.
Amen.

Lord, when I walk in darkness
be my light.
When I lose hold on you
keep me in your firm grip.
When I am troubled
give me your peace.
When I am weary
breathe into me the power of your Spirit,
that I may witness to you
and your resurrection.
Amen.

When we do wrong

God, help me to do what is good
and to walk in the right ways.
When I do wrong
may I turn again to what you want me to do.
Guide me by your presence
and protect me with your love,
that I may walk in the way that leads me to you.
Amen.

Lord, help me to love you
with all my heart, mind and soul.
Forgive me when I am led astray
and deliver me from evil.
Amen.

Holy and ever-loving God,
thank you for the forgiveness of sins
and the opportunity to start anew.
I pray that you will fill my heart
with your goodness
and my mind with your love.
Amen.

Lord God,
on the way of goodness,
when I fall,
forgive me and lift me up.
Help me to do your will
and to seek to bring in your kingdom.
Give me the strength to resist temptation
and to do what is right and good.
Amen.

God, thank you for your love.
When I am down you lift me up,
when I stray you seek to bring me back,
when I fail you forgive me.
Lord, help me to lead a useful life
and to serve you faithfully.
Amen.

God, thank you for the forgiveness of sins
and the opportunity to start again.
I am sorry for when I have done wrong
and gone against your love.
Forgive me and help me to do better.
Amen.

Lord, on the way of goodness,
if I stumble, help me and bring me back.
Give me the courage to stand against evil
and to seek what is good.
May I seek your will
and work for the coming of your kingdom.
Amen.

Lord God, you forgive me
when I stray away from you
and you seek me with love.
Lord, I turn to you
and give my love to you this day.
Amen.

Lord God,
help me not to be overcome with evil
but to overcome evil with good.
May I be known as a loving
and forgiving person,
someone with a kind heart
and a generous spirit.
Amen.

Lord Jesus, I am sorry
when I have lost contact with you,
when I have forgotten my prayers
or thought I was too busy.
I seek your presence and your healing power
in my life.
Amen.

Lord Jesus,
you gave your life in obedience to the Father
that we might live in the fullness
of your kingdom.
Keep me faithful and true to you
and help me to resist all temptation.
Amen.

Lord God,
you are always more ready to hear
than I am to pray.
Forgive me when I have been deaf to your call
and when I have failed to proclaim you to others.
Open my ears to hear your word to me
and my lips to sing your praises.
Amen.

Also available:

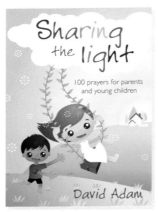

Sharing the light
1501102

The best way to show your child that you believe in God
is to talk to God in their presence and to encourage
them to talk to God in their own simple words.

The prayers in this book are to assist your own prayers
and your child's. Spend a little time together each day
simply rejoicing in the presence and turning to the light
and love of God. Say the prayers together so that they
are not simply recited but learnt by heart – that is,
learnt by worship and not by the mind alone.

Prayer is a great adventure and the opening of
our lives to the love and light of our God.
Enjoy that adventure with your child.

Walking in the light
1501103

When we pray we turn to our God who loves us
and cares for us. God wants us to share
with him all that we do.

These prayers are to help you know that God loves
you and is with you. Make a special time and place
each day to say your prayers. Spend some time in
silence just knowing that God is with you and that he
loves you, and then use a prayer and let the prayer
encourage you to pray words of your own.

By praying we learn to walk in the light
and love of God.